FUN·TO·MAKE CRAFTS FOR HALLOWEEN

Boyds Mills Press

Editor

Tom Daning

Craft Contributors

Robin Adams	Janet Grottodden	Lauren Michaels	Bonnie Wedge
Barbara Baker	Jean Hale	Judi Miskell	Margaret Joque Williams
B. J. Benish	Edna Harrington	Beatrice Bachrach Perri	Agnes Choate Wonson
Linda Bloomgren	Barbara Albers Hill	James W. Perrin Jr.	D. A. Woodliff
Norma Jean Byrkett	Joan Holmes	Deanna Peters	
Marie Cecchini	Velma Flower Holt	Jean Reynolds	
Mindy Cherez	Cameron Horn	Terry A. Ricioli	
Diana Conley	Helen Jeffries	Kathy Ross	
Liby Croce	Susan Jensen	Laura Sassi	
Marie Crouch	Tama Kain	Vivian Smallowitz	
Sandra Csippan	Garnett Kooker	Andrew Smith	
Ruth Dougherty	Jean Kuhn	Barbara Smith	
Kathy Everett	Twilla Lamm	Cheryl Stees	
Tanya Turner Fry	Lee Lindeman	Debora Sullivan	
Monica M. Graham	Doreen Macklen	Marilyn Thomason	
Mavis Grant	Agnes Maddy	Sherry Timberman	
Evelyn Green	Jo Ann Markway	Sharon Dunn Umnik	

Craft Builder

Verlie Hutchens

Copyright © 2005 by Boyds Mills Press
All rights reserved

Published by Boyds Mills Press, Inc.
A Highlights Company
815 Church Street
Honesdale, Pennsylvania 18431
Printed in China

Publisher Cataloging-in-Publication Data

Fun-to-make crafts for Halloween / Boyds Mills Press.—1st ed.
[64] p.: col. photos. ; cm.
Includes index.
Summary: Includes step-by-step directions to make decorations, gifts, and
    greeting cards for Halloween.
ISBN 1-59078-343-3
ISBN 1-59078-368-9 (pbk.)
1. Halloween decorations. 2. Handicraft. I. Title.
745.594 22   TT900.F86h 2005

First edition, 2005
Book designed by Janet Moir McCaffrey
The text of this book is set in 11-point New Century Schoolbook.

Visit our Web site at www.boydsmillspress.com

10 9 8 7 6 5 4 3 2 1 hc
10 9 8 7 6 5 4 3 2 1 pb

*I*n these pages you will find more than 140 imaginative craft ideas for Halloween and fall. Gifts, games, toys, decorations, greeting cards—whatever you want to make, it's here. So put on your most stylish paint-splattered smock, roll up your sleeves, and create. Soon ghosts, goblins, and witches will be at your door!

Safety First

Although most crafts in this book are designed for you to make yourself, remember to ask for an adult's help when handling sharp instruments or using the stove.

Follow the Directions— But Add Your Own Flair

To build each craft, follow the steps listed. The directions and the pictures are helpful guides, but they are no substitute for your own imagination. You might figure out a different way to make a witch's hat or to decorate your jack-o'-lantern. Or you might be inspired to make up your own crafts.

Neatness Counts

Before you get crafty, be smart and cover your work area. Old newspapers, brown paper bags, old sheets, or a plastic drop cloth will work. Protect your clothes with an apron, a smock, or a big old shirt. And remember to clean up after you are finished.

Stock Your Craft Workshop

We've included a list of materials to make each craft. Recyclable items such as cardboard tubes, plastic milk bottles, and paper bags are needed for many of them. Before you start, check out the items in the materials list for the crafts you plan to make. Ask your parents, friends, and relatives to start saving these things for you, so you will always have a supply on hand. If you don't have the exact item listed, something else may work just as well. Make sure you clean and dry the recyclables before using them. Also, good crafters usually keep some supplies handy—such as scissors, crayons, markers, craft glue, tape, pens, pencils, paint, a hole punch, and a stapler. Because these are used so frequently, we don't include them in the list of materials. Several crafts call for papier-mâché. For directions on making papier-mâché, see Pumpkin Sculpture, page 8.

Have Fun!

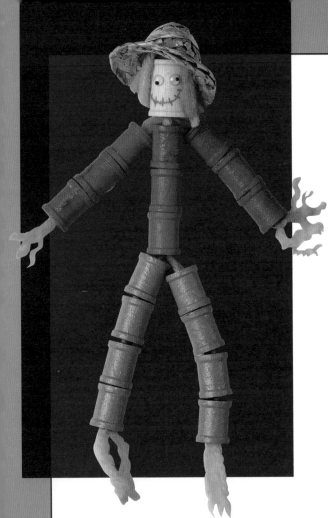

Floppy Scarecrow

small wooden spools ● yarn ● tiny straw hat
● wiggle eyes ● red permanent marker

1. Paint eight small wooden spools blue and nine red. Let dry. Leave one spool unpainted.
2. Cut eight strands of yarn, and knot them together at one end. Thread all yarn pieces through the unpainted spool. (You may need to use a chenille stick to help thread the yarn through.)
3. Separate the strands (two for each arm and four for the body). Thread three red spools onto each arm and onto the middle body strands. Thread four blue spools onto each leg made of two strands. Knot each arm and leg and fray the yarn ends.
4. Glue a hat to the top of the head and wiggle eyes onto the face. Let dry.
5. Use a permanent marker to draw a smile.

Apple-y Greetings

apple ● paper towel ● white and colored paper

1. With an adult's help, cut an apple in half lengthwise. Blot the cut side of one half with a paper towel, and set it aside for a few minutes to dry out a little.
2. Paint the cut side of the slightly dry apple. Press it onto a sheet of white paper. Let dry.
3. Glue paper cutout decorations to the print: a stem and leaf for an apple or a stem and features for a jack-o'-lantern.
4. Glue the white paper to a slightly larger piece of colored paper. Glue that to the front of a sheet of folded paper to make the card.
5. Write an autumn or Halloween greeting inside the card.

Hangin' with Mr. Spider

film canister ● yarn ● felt ● paper

1. With an adult's help, use a ballpoint pen to poke a hole in the bottom of a film canister.
2. Thread yarn through the hole, and make a large knot at the end inside the canister.
3. For legs, cut four 7-inch-by-½-inch strips of felt. Spread glue around the inside edge of the canister lid. Place the legs on the lid (over the glue) so that their centers overlap in the middle. Squeeze glue around the open edge of the canister, then push it hard into the lid.
4. Make eyes from paper, and glue them on. Hang your spider by the yarn or make him dance along the floor.

Chenille-Stick Bones

chenille sticks ● paper ● thread

1. Bend a long chenille stick in half. Below the bend, twist a second chenille stick around for the arms.
2. Just below the arms, wrap a third chenille stick around the first for the body, leaving two lengths for the legs.
3. Cut out a paper head and glue it to the body. Bend back the ends of the arms and legs to make the hands and feet.
4. Add a thread loop to the head, and jiggle it to make the skeleton dance.

Shiny Trick-or-Treat Bag

brown paper bag ● aluminum foil ● foam paper ● yarn

1. Fold over the top of a brown paper bag several times to make a cuff. Decorate the bag with a jack-o'-lantern cut from aluminum foil. Add foam-paper features. Glue a strip of foil to the top.

A B C

2. To make the braided handle, cut three pieces of yarn the same length. Line up the pieces, and tie them together in a knot about 1 inch from one end. Braid by folding A over B and then C over A. Continue until the yarn is braided. Tie the ends into a knot again about 1 inch from the end.

A
B C

3. Staple the handle ends to the sides of the bag.

Spooky Sock

old white sock ● newspaper ● craft stick
● black permanent marker ● yarn

1. Cut several slits in the leg section of an old white sock.
2. Wad up a sheet of newspaper, and stuff it into the foot of the sock. Place a craft stick crosswise in the sock. Then stuff more newspaper in the sock to hold the craft stick in place. Continue to stuff in more newspaper until you have filled the entire foot of the sock.
3. Make a face with black permanent marker. With a pencil, poke two holes at the top of the ghost's head and pull a piece of yarn through them. Tie the ends together, and hang the ghost in a breezy place.

Wobbler

heavy paper plate ● plastic bottle cap ● utility knife ● small orange plastic egg
● hot-glue gun ● self-adhesive label

1. In the center of a heavy paper plate, trace a circle using a plastic bottle cap as a guide. Ask an adult to make four cuts in the circle, creating eight wedges. Press the wedges through the cut area to open the circle. Place the plastic cap snugly in the hole so the inside of the cap faces up. Turn the plate over and tape the cap to the pushed-through wedges.
2. Paint the plate as desired.
3. Ask an adult to fill the smaller half of an orange plastic egg with glue from a hot-glue gun. This will make the pumpkin wobble. Use hot glue to seal the egg.
4. Color a self-adhesive label black and cut out the features of two jack-o'-lanterns, one happy, one sad. Press the features on opposite sides of the egg.
5. To play, hold the plate by the cap underneath. Try to get the wobbling pumpkin into the hole. To keep score, give yourself a point for each time you land the pumpkin's smiling face toward you. Take away a point for each time you land the sad face toward you.

Dangling Spider

black thread ● large plastic-foam ball
● chenille sticks ● wiggle eyes

1. Cut a length of heavy black thread about 3 feet long. Tie one end of it around a large plastic-foam ball.
2. Paint the ball black. Let dry.
3. Cut four black chenille sticks in half. Poke one end of each half into the ball and bend the chenille sticks to look like the spider's legs.
4. Glue on wiggle eyes.
5. Hang the spider from a doorway or window.

Halloween Treat Bag

construction paper ● large brown paper bag

1. Glue a half-sheet of construction paper on each wide side of a large brown paper bag as shown. Let dry.
2. Draw a handle on each piece of paper, across the center of the bag. Cut around the outside and inside of the handles and around the sides of the bag. (See diagram.)
3. Use crayons, markers, or cut paper to decorate the outside of the bag.

Frances Felt

two copper scouring pads ● pumpkin
● toothpicks ● felt ● pompoms ● lace

1. For the hair, stretch two copper scouring pads over the top of a pumpkin. Hold in place with toothpick halves.
2. Cut eyes, a nose, a mouth, cheeks, and ears from felt. Roll pieces of tape and attach to the back of the features. Press the features in place. Glue a pompom on each lobe for an earring.
3. Add a felt-and-lace bow to the hair. Hold in place with a toothpick half. Wrap a strip of lace around the neck.

Pumpkin Sculpture

papier-mâché (flour and water, white paper towels)
● round balloon ● heavy cardboard ● construction paper

1. To make papier-mâché, mix flour and water together until it is the consistency of ketchup. Dip strips of white paper towels into the flour mixture. Place a layer of strips on an inflated round balloon and let dry. Add another layer and let dry.
2. To make the pumpkin, cut a section from the bottom of the round shape so it will sit level and not roll away. Cover with paint and let dry.
3. To make the base, cut a rectangular piece of heavy cardboard. Cut various leaf shapes from construction paper and glue on top. Glue the pumpkin to the center.
4. Add a paper stem, leaves, and vines to the decoration.

Skeleton Hand

black chenille sticks ● clear and white beads

1. Hold five black chenille sticks together tightly. Thread beads over all five chenille sticks, leaving several inches unbeaded at the end. Bend the other end to hold the beads in place.
2. Spread the unbeaded chenille sticks into fingers and thread beads onto each finger, bending the end of each chenille stick to hold the beads in place. Shape fingers into a claw.

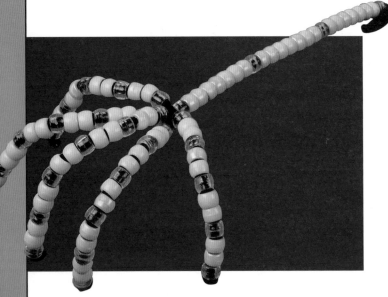

Panda Mask

large, heavy white paper plate ● construction paper
● lightweight cardboard ● cardboard tube

1. Draw a panda face on the bottom of a large, heavy white paper plate. Cut out holes for eyes and a small mouth. Glue a red tongue cut from construction paper near the mouth.
2. Cut ears from lightweight cardboard and paint them black. Staple them to the plate with the smooth section of the staple inside.
3. Cover a cardboard tube with black construction paper and fasten with tape. Staple the tube to one side of the panda face for a handle.

Baggy Scarecrow

one medium-sized and one small brown paper bag
● brown paper ● newspaper ● construction paper
● straw hat

1. For the body, use a medium-sized brown paper bag. For the arms, roll a few sheets of brown paper into a tube. Poke a hole in each side of the bag near the top, and push the arms through. Stuff the body with crumpled newspaper, fold the opening closed, and staple it shut.
2. For the head, use a small paper bag stuffed with newspaper. Twist and tape the bag shut. Make a small hole in the body and insert the twisted end of the head into the hole. Use tape to hold it in place.
3. Roll a few sheets of brown paper into two small tubes for the legs. Poke two holes in the bottom of the body and insert the legs. Add tape to hold them in place.
4. Glue on cut paper for features and patches. Cut and glue paper for the feet, hands, neck, and head. Add an old straw hat.

"Purr"-fect Pet

old sock ● thread ● felt ● foam paper

1. Gather material on each side of the toe portion of an old sock for the ears. Tie the ears with thread.
2. Cut out eyes, a nose, and whiskers from felt and foam paper, and glue them in place on the foot of the sock.
3. Place your hand inside the sock to make your cat perform.

Pumpkin Collage

construction paper
● clear self-adhesive paper
● green ribbon

1. From construction paper, cut out orange circles, green pumpkin stems, and black facial features.
2. Cut out two 10-inch squares from clear self-adhesive paper. Peel the paper off one square. Lay it flat on the table, sticky side up.
3. Place the orange circles randomly over the sticky square. Place the pumpkin faces on top of the circles. Put the stems above the eyes.
4. Peel the paper off the second square and place the sticky side over the pumpkin collage. Smooth it down, pushing out any air bubbles.
5. Trace a 9-inch circle on your square collage, and cut it out. Using a hole punch, make a hole at the top of the circle. Thread green ribbon through the hole for a hanger. Hang your pumpkin collage in a window.

Owl Bag

small brown paper bag ● newspaper ● construction paper ● self-adhesive reinforcement rings

1. Stuff a small brown paper bag half full of crumpled newspaper.
2. Bring the top of the bag together, fold the two outside edges in toward the center, and glue to form a point.
3. Fold the point down over the bag and glue in place.
4. From construction paper, make a beak and glue to the point. Make feet and glue them to the bottom of the bag. Add two self-adhesive reinforcement rings for eyes.

Sun Mask

large, heavy paper plate
● lightweight cardboard
● papier-mâché ● elastic

1. Use the outside bottom of a large, heavy paper plate for the sun. To make rays, cut triangles from lightweight cardboard, and staple them around the sun.
2. Cover the entire sun with papier-mâché, adding rolled pieces of papier-mâché to create eyebrows and a mouth. Let dry.
3. Paint and let dry. Cut out eyeholes. Staple elastic to opposite sides of the mask to fit around your head.

"Phantastic" Game

shoebox and lid ● three Ping-Pong balls ● white paper ● large wooden spool

1. Remove the lid from an empty shoebox. Paint the inside of the lid with black paint and let dry. Paint three Ping-Pong balls orange and let dry. Add pumpkin features with black paint.
2. Draw a ghost shape on a piece of white paper to fit inside the lid. Cut out the ghost and glue it inside the lid.
3. To make the eyes and mouth, place a large wooden spool on the face and trace around the spool. Cut along the outline. Turn the shoebox upside down, and hold the lid against the bottom. Trace around the holes for the eyes and mouth, then cut along the outlines.
4. Glue the lid to the bottom of the box, matching the holes. Cut out sections of the sides of the shoebox to make legs.
5. Drop the three balls onto the lid. Hold the box in your hands, and roll the balls around until you have filled the holes.

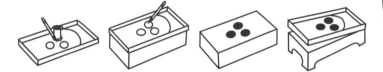

Black-Cat Basket

ribbon ● plastic berry basket
● poster board

1. Start at a corner and weave lengths of ribbon in and out through the sections of a plastic berry basket. Tie each ribbon into a bow at the end.
2. From a piece of poster board, cut out the head of a cat with a long neck. Decorate it with pieces of poster board and markers.
3. Cut small slits in the neck section and weave them into the berry basket sections at the corner above the bows. Fill the basket with treats.

"Lights Out" Pumpkin

construction paper

1. Fold a 1-foot strip of orange construction paper into three equal sections. Trim the sides of the paper to form a pumpkin, but do not cut the folds.
2. Unfold the paper and cut out eyes, a nose, and a mouth in the center section, making a pumpkin face.
3. Cover the top section with yellow construction paper and the bottom section with black.
4. Fold again, with the pumpkin facing you. Glue on a paper stem. Add lines with a marker or crayon to outline the pumpkin.
5. Fold so that the yellow paper shows through the pumpkin face when it is "on" and the black shows through when it is "off."

Bear Mask

small, heavy paper bowl
● large, heavy paper plate
● lightweight cardboard
● papier-mâché ● elastic

1. To make the bear's snout, turn over a small, heavy paper bowl, and place it on top of the outside bottom of a large, heavy paper plate. Tape it on the plate. Cut small ears from pieces of lightweight cardboard, and staple them to the plate.
2. Cover the mask with papier-mâché, adding rolled pieces of papier-mâché to form the eyebrows. Let dry.
3. Paint and let dry. Add features with paint. Let dry. Cut out eyeholes. Staple a piece of elastic to opposite sides of the mask to fit around your head.

Pin-On Witch

lightweight cardboard
- black and yellow construction paper
- dried wheat stalk ● safety pin

1. Cut out two 2½-inch circles, one from lightweight cardboard and one from black construction paper. Glue them together.
2. Cut a slightly smaller circle from yellow construction paper and glue it to the center of the black circle.
3. From black paper, draw and cut out a witch that will fit on the yellow circle.
4. Use a dried wheat stalk for a broom and glue it to the yellow circle. Glue the witch on top of the broom.
5. Glue a small safety pin to the back.

Felt-Rat Scissor Case

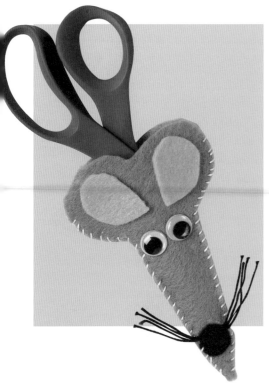

paper ● felt ● embroidery floss ● wiggle eyes ● needle

1. Trace your mom's favorite pair of scissors on a piece of paper. Add a ½-inch margin around the shape and cut it out. Lay your pattern on gray felt and cut out two pieces.
2. Decorate one of the gray pieces to look like a rat. Cut ears from pink felt and a nose from black felt. Snip embroidery floss to look like whiskers. Glue everything in place and let dry. Add wiggle eyes.
3. Place the two pieces together with the face on top. Sew the pieces together, leaving the ears end open.
4. Give this to your mom as a gift on Halloween.

Pumpkin-Patch Pals

pebbles ● stick of wood

1. To make pumpkins, wash and dry small round, flat pebbles. Paint them orange and create faces.
2. Use long, flat pebbles for the ghosts. Paint them white and create faces.
3. Glue the pumpkins and ghosts to a small stick of wood.

Paper Spider

black paper ● two small paper plates ● string

1. Cut eight long strips of black paper for the spider's legs and a circle for the spider's head.
2. Glue the two small paper plates together, plate bottoms facing out, with the legs and head placed between the edges.
3. Paint the body black. Glue a long piece of string to the middle of the back so the spider can dangle from the ceiling.

Tree of Trolls

cream containers ● construction paper ● fallen tree branch ● plastic food container ● modeling clay ● fabric ● yarn ● string

1. For each troll, glue together two small cream containers. Cut features from construction paper and other materials to decorate each troll.
2. Stick a fallen tree branch into a plastic food container filled with modeling clay. Cut a circle of fabric. Wrap it around the container and tie it together with yarn.
3. Glue a piece of string to the top of each troll, and tie the trolls to the branches.

Pig Mask

heavy cardboard ● pink construction paper ● wooden spool ● large craft stick

1. Draw and cut out two 9-inch circles, one from heavy cardboard and one from pink construction paper. Cut two ears from pink paper, and glue them to the cardboard circle. Glue the pink circle to the front of the cardboard circle.
2. Draw two circles for the pig's eyes, and cut them out. Paint a wooden spool pink for the snout and glue it on. Use a marker to draw on a mouth and add other details.
3. Paint a large craft stick and let dry. Glue the craft stick to one side of the pig's head to use as a holder.

Yummy Creepy Crawlers

chocolate sandwich cookies ● chocolate frosting ● licorice ● round candies

1. For each treat, gently separate a chocolate sandwich cookie. Spread chocolate frosting over the half without the cream filling and set it aside. Put the half with the cream filling in front of you.
2. Cut licorice into 2-inch pieces. Press the ends of eight licorice pieces into the cream filling to make the legs (four on each side).
3. Gently place the cookie half with the chocolate frosting (frosting-side down) over the legs.
4. For eyes, use frosting to attach two round candies to the top of the cookie.

Scarecrow Magnet

felt ● cardboard ● yellow yarn ● magnetic strip

1. Cut out two scarecrow shapes from felt and one from cardboard. Glue them together with the cardboard in between the felt pieces.
2. To make the front of the scarecrow, glue yarn pieces on the wrists, ankles, and head.
3. Cut out clothes and facial features from felt and glue in place.
4. Glue a magnetic strip onto the back.

Rat Hat

construction paper ● felt ● chenille stick

1. Cut out a 9-inch square of construction paper for the hat. Fold it into a triangle.
2. To make the band, cut a strip of paper 11½ inches long and 1½ inches wide. Glue the band to each of the corners opposite the fold.
3. Glue on features made from circles of cut paper or felt. For the tail, staple a curled chenille stick to the top corner.

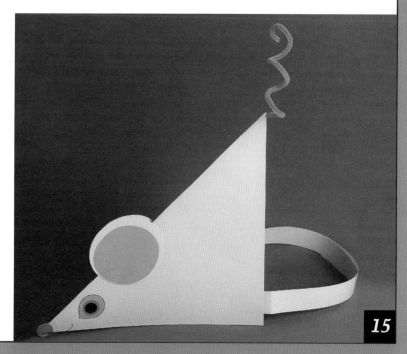

Freddie Fruit Face

two apples ● cucumber
● pumpkin ● table knife ● toothpicks
● marshmallows ● paper ● celery

1. Cut two apples and a cucumber in half. On the pumpkin surface, trace around one top-half section of the apple for the mouth, two bottom-half sections of the apples for the cheeks, and one half of the cucumber for the nose. Cut around the tracings with a table knife, cutting through the pumpkin wall, and push the apple halves and cucumber inside the pumpkin.
2. Insert two toothpicks where the eyes should be, and place a marshmallow on each one. Add a pupil made from paper to each eye. For the eyebrows, cut small sections from the leftover cucumber and attach them with toothpick halves.
3. Cut the leafy sections from a bunch of celery. Attach them with toothpick halves to the top of the pumpkin to make hair.

Owl Family

lightweight cardboard ● brown paper bag
● construction paper ● yarn ● pinecones

1. Cut an owl head from lightweight cardboard. Cover it with a piece of brown paper bag. Trim around the edges. Add two big round eyes and a triangular beak from construction paper.
2. Punch a hole at the top between the eyes, and add a loop of yarn for a hanger.
3. Glue eyes and a beak on each of four pinecones to make little owls. Glue a piece of yarn to the top of each one.
4. Punch two holes on each side of the big owl's beak. Tie a little owl to each hole.

Five Little Pumpkins

cardboard egg carton ● construction paper

1. Cut ten cups from a cardboard egg carton. Glue them together in pairs to make five pumpkins. Paint them orange.
2. Cut a section of five peaks from the egg carton for the bases. Trim the peaks to make them different heights. Paint the bases black.
3. Glue one pumpkin to each base. Attach cut-paper features to the pumpkins.

Treat Cups

paper cups ● chenille sticks ● yarn ● felt

1. For each cup, punch two holes across from each other near the top of a paper cup. To make the handles, twist two chenille sticks together. Place the ends of the chenille stick through the holes in the cup. Fold up and twist the ends of the chenille stick.
2. Spread glue on the top inch of the cup and wrap yarn around it. Little by little, continue gluing and wrapping until the entire cup is covered.
3. Cut out eyes, a nose, a mouth, and other decorations from felt. Glue them on.

Candy-Corn Place Card

white poster board

1. On a piece of white poster board, draw and cut out the shape shown in the diagram.
2. Color the cutout to look like a giant piece of candy corn. Add a guest's name with a marker.
3. Fold as shown in the picture and glue together. Make one for each of your guests.

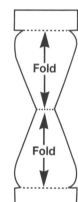

Fold

Fold

JOSÉ

Kitty Cat Mask

large, heavy paper plate ● lightweight cardboard
● papier-mâché ● paper ● elastic

1. With the outside bottom of a large, heavy paper plate facing up, trim the plate to form the cat's head. Cut ears from lightweight cardboard and staple in place. Cover with papier-mâché.
2. To make the nose and cheeks, cover small wads of paper with papier-mâché. Add a small papier-mâché tongue. Let dry.
3. Add features with paint. Cut out eyeholes, and staple elastic to opposite sides of the mask to fit around your head.

Itsy-Bitsy Spider

chenille stick ● yarn ● wiggle eyes

1. Cut a chenille stick into four equal pieces.
2. To make the eight legs, cross the pieces at their centers.
3. Cut a 30-inch-long piece of yarn, and tie one end around the center, where the legs meet.
4. To make the body, wrap the yarn around the center. Leave about 10 inches as a hanger, and tie a knot to hold the yarn in place.
5. Bend the legs. Glue on wiggle eyes.

Oopsy-Daisy Witch

small cardboard tube ● chenille sticks ● construction paper ● wiggle eyes ● yarn

1. Pinch the top of a small cardboard tube and glue the ends together. Round the top edges. Cut a small hole on each side. Trim the bottom of the tube into a ragged edge. Paint the tube black and let dry.
2. Twist together one green and one purple chenille stick. Repeat this step to make two green-and-purple chenille sticks.
3. Twist the chenille sticks together at the center, making an X shape. Thread two ends up the tube and into the holes. Bend up the ends to make arms.
4. Cut out hair from orange construction paper and a face and two hands from green construction paper. From black paper cut a hat. Draw details on the face and add wiggle eyes. Glue the head in place and glue shoes to the end of the legs.
5. Bend a brown chenille stick in half and around some pieces of gold yarn. Twist the halves together to make a broom. Bend the witch's hands over the broomstick and glue them in place.

18

Ghost Pop-Out Card

construction paper ● plastic-foam tray

1. For the card, fold a piece of construction paper in half. Fold it over in half again the other way.
2. Decorate the front of the card with cut pieces of paper. Write a greeting on another piece of paper, and glue it to the inside of the card.
3. Cut out a ghost from a plastic-foam tray and add paper eyes.
4. Cut two strips of paper 1 inch wide and fold them over each other in the direction shown to form a paper spring. Glue the spring to the card and the back of the ghost.

1. 2. 3.

4. 5.

Witch Mask

cardboard candy box ● papier-mâché ● paper ● elastic

1. Use the outside of a cardboard candy box with a lid to create the witch. Cut and tape together as shown.
2. Cover the box and lid with papier-mâché. To make the nose, cover a wad of paper with papier-mâché. Add strips of papier-mâché to create eyebrows and a mouth. Fold a strip of papier-mâché for cheeks.
3. Paint the features and let dry. Cut out eyeholes. Staple a piece of elastic to opposite sides of the mask to fit around your head.

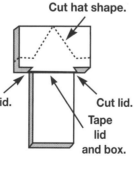

Cut hat shape.

Cut lid.

Cut lid.

Tape lid and box.

Paper-Plate Owl

paper plate ● construction paper

1. Cut along the inside of a paper plate's fluted edge, except for 2 inches on the top and bottom as shown.
2. Fold the two cut edges inward so that they overlap, and glue them down.
3. Color the owl with markers. Cut eyes, ears, feet, and a beak from construction paper and glue them in place.

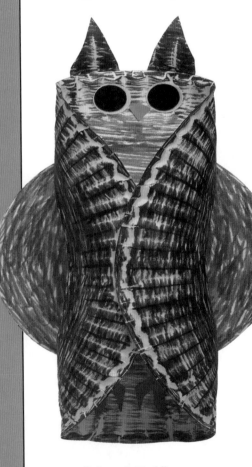

Cut on dotted line.

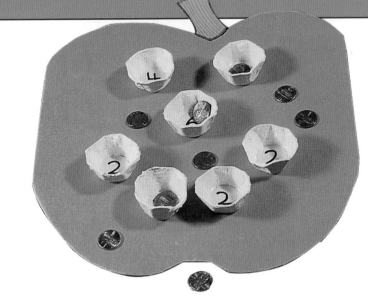

Pumpkin-Patch Pitch

cardboard ● construction paper ● cardboard egg carton

1. Draw and cut out a large pumpkin shape from cardboard. Cover the shape with orange construction paper. Color the stem with a marker or paint.
2. Trim seven cardboard egg-carton sections to make little cups. Paint the cups yellow, then glue them to the pumpkin to make a jack-o'-lantern face.
3. Cut smaller paper circles to fit inside each egg-carton cup. Write a point value on each circle, then glue one circle into the bottom of each cup.
4. When the glue is dry, take turns tossing pennies onto the pumpkin. To find your score, add the numbers on the cups in which your pennies land.

Tiny Spider

wiggle eyes ● pompom ● small plastic toy container ● yarn

1. Glue two wiggle eyes to a black and orange pompom. Stuff the pompom into a small plastic toy container with the eyes facing out.
2. Lay four strands of black yarn across the opening of the container. Snap the lid over the yarn.

Pint-Sized Goblin

pint-sized ice-cream container ● felt ● cardboard

1. Cover a pint-sized ice-cream container with felt.
2. Cut a bottom with feet from cardboard, cover with felt, and glue in place.
3. Cut out arms and scary facial features from felt and glue them to your goblin.

Bat Pencil Topper

rubber eraser cap ● pencil ● permanent marker ● construction paper

1. Place a rubber eraser cap on the top of a pencil. With scissors, cut out a small notch at the top of the eraser to form two pointed ears.
2. Color the eraser black with a permanent marker.
3. Cut out bat wings from construction paper. Glue the wings to the back of the eraser and let dry. Cut out small paper eyes, and glue them to the bat.

1. Cut 1½".
2. Staple.
3. Glue and tape handle.

Caterpillar Mask

large, heavy paper plates ● poster board ● yarn

1. Paint the bottoms of four large, heavy paper plates and let dry.
2. Make a face on one plate with pieces of poster board and glue. Cut out holes for the eyes, draw eyelashes, and staple on antennae.
3. Cut legs from poster board and staple them opposite each other on the plates. Add dots cut from poster board.
4. To connect the body, punch two holes, about 1 inch apart, at the edge of the plate where the neck would be. Punch two holes in another plate so the holes line up. Place the holes over each other and tie with a piece of yarn. Do the same with the rest of the plates.
5. Cut a 1½-inch section from the center of a fifth plate. (See diagram above.) Cut in half, overlap, and staple together. Attach the handle over the neck area on the underside.

Torn-Paper Owl Bank

plastic container with lid ● construction paper

1. Ask an adult to cut a quarter-sized slot about 1½ inches from the bottom of a plastic container.
2. Cover the container with black construction paper. Gently reopen the slot with scissors.
3. Rip a scrap of orange paper to look like an owl's face. Glue it in place over the coin slot. Use scissors to open the slot again.
4. Rip white and black paper to look like an open eye. Glue in place. Glue on torn-paper lashes under the slot to look like a winking eye. Add lashes to the other eye. Rip red paper to look like feet and glue at the bottom of the face. Cover the sides and back of the bank with torn-paper feathers.
5. Snap on the lid and start collecting coins.

Invisible Ghost Card

construction paper ● wax crayons ● watercolor paint

1. Fold a piece of white construction paper in half to make a card.
2. Use crayons to draw an October scene. Press hard. Leave space to add your "invisible" ghost.
3. Use a white wax crayon to draw the outline of your ghost. Color the ghost in completely with the white crayon.
4. Inside the card, use a pen to write: "Paint this card with watercolor blue to find a ghost playing peek-a-boo!"
5. Give the card to a friend. When he or she paints the front, the ghost will suddenly appear.

Two-Faced Cat

one-pint milk carton ● cardboard

1. Use a one-pint milk carton for the cat, with the opened peaks forming the ears. Draw the eyes and mouth on the side of the carton and cut them out. Paint the carton and let dry.
2. Cut a slit in the bottom of the carton below the cat's face. Cut a strip of cardboard as wide as the carton and as long as needed to reach the carton top. Place the strip in the slit and trace the eyes and mouth on it.
3. Paint the eyes on the cardboard strip. Draw a long tongue on another piece of cardboard that will fit inside the cat's mouth. Cut it out and paint it. Glue one end of the tongue to the strip of cardboard so the other end of the tongue can slide in and out of the mouth.
4. Hold the carton with one hand and the cardboard strip with the other. Make the cat's tongue and eyes move up and down.

Chick Mask

large paper bag ● construction paper

1. Measure about 6 inches from the opening of a large paper bag, and cut around the entire bag. Set aside the cut section.
2. Put the bag on your head. Using a crayon, have a friend carefully mark where the eyeholes should be on the outside of the bag. Remove the bag.
3. Cut out and glue facial features on the chick from construction paper, but make large eyes. Cut holes for eyes. Add curled strips of paper to the top of the chick head.

Tracy the Skeleton

poster board ● wooden spoon ● scissors
● heart-shaped candy ● cotton swab ● screw ● key

1. On poster board, trace around a wooden spoon, a pair of closed scissors, a large heart-shaped candy, a cotton swab (fourteen times), a screw (eight times), and a key (four times). Cut out the shapes.
2. Glue the point of the scissors shape to the handle of the spoon shape. The spoon will be the head. Draw a face on it.
3. Glue the heart on the scissors below the head. Glue on six cotton swab shapes as ribs. For each arm and leg, glue together two cotton swab shapes end to end. Glue them onto the body.
4. To make each hand, glue four screw shapes onto a key shape. Glue the hands on the ends of the arms. To make feet, glue a key shape onto the end of each leg.

"Fab" Pumpkin

pizza pan ● fabric ● needle and thread

1. Place a pizza pan on a piece of orange fabric. Trace around it with a pencil and cut out the circle.
2. Sew around the edge of the circle using long stitches. When you get all the way around, pull the thread ends to gather the fabric, leaving a small hole in the center.
3. Stuff old fabric scraps into the hole, forming the pumpkin shape. Roll green fabric into a stem and push it into the hole.
4. Pull the thread very tightly and secure with a few stitches. Glue on pieces of fabric to make a face. Sew on fabric leaves.

Ghostly Jinglers

one-gallon plastic milk jug ● thread ● jingle bells

1. Cut ghost shapes from the sides of a one-gallon plastic milk jug.
2. Using a hole punch, make eyeholes in each ghost. With a pen, punch a hole in the top of each ghost, and tie a thread loop for a hanger.
3. Poke a small hole with a pen at the bottom of each ghost. Place a small jingle bell on a piece of thread, and tie it to the bottom of each ghost.
4. Hang the ghosts where the wind will make them flutter and the bells jingle.

Flying Pumpkins

chenille sticks ● construction paper
● cardboard egg carton ● large and small craft sticks
● green electrical tape ● soda bottle cap
● rubber band ● pompoms

1. Twist the ends of two green chenille sticks together, making one long chenille stick. Bend the chenille stick into a twisting vine design. Cut out four leaf shapes from green construction paper and glue them to the vine, spacing them out evenly.
3. Cut out four cups from a cardboard egg carton and paint them green. When dry, glue them to the tops of the leaves.
4. To make a launcher, glue three small craft sticks together, and let dry. Glue the three sticks across a large craft stick, about 1 inch from the end. Let dry. Paint all of the craft sticks as desired.
5. Wrap green electrical tape around the sides of a soda bottle cap. Glue the cap to the end of a large craft stick. Place the large craft sticks together and wrap the ends with a rubber band as shown.
6. To play Flying Pumpkins, place a pompom "pumpkin" in the launcher and try to land it in the pumpkin patch.

Trick-or-Treat Box

milk carton ● construction paper ● yarn

1. Cut the top from a milk carton, leaving an open box. Cover the sides with glue and construction paper.
2. Decorate the box with cutouts from construction paper to make funny and scary faces.
3. Punch a hole on opposite sides at the top of the box. To make a handle, thread two pieces of yarn through the holes and knot the ends.

Mr. Beans the Cat

poster board ● black beans ● pumpkin seeds ● dried green peas ● kidney beans ● broom straw ● needle and thread

1. Draw and cut out a cat shape from black poster board. Glue on black beans for the body.
2. Add pumpkin seeds and dried green peas for eyes. Use a pumpkin seed for a nose and two kidney beans for a mouth. Cut small pieces of broom straw for whiskers.
3. Let all the seeds and beans dry. With a needle and thread, poke a hole between the beans at the top of the cat. Remove the needle. Then knot the ends of the thread to make a hanger.

Mouse Mask

large, heavy paper plate ● three small paper plates ● papier-mâché ● elastic

1. Use the outside bottom of a large, heavy paper plate for the face of the mouse. To make ears, staple two small paper plates, right-side up, to the large plate.
2. To make the nose, cut a small section from a small paper plate as shown. Bend it to form the point of a nose, and tape it in place on the face. Cover the nose, ears, and face with papier-mâché and let dry.

Cut on dotted line.

3. Add features with paint, and let dry. Cut out eyeholes. Staple a piece of elastic to opposite sides of the mask to fit around your head and knot the ends.

26

Wall Shadows

tracing paper ● plastic trash bag

1. Draw a Halloween shape on a piece of tracing paper.
2. Hold the paper up to a window with the design facing outside. Trace around your design with a glue stick. Set aside until almost dry but still slightly tacky.
3. Cut a sheet of black or white plastic from a trash bag and press it onto the glued side of the paper. Turn it over and cut along the line you drew.
4. Peel the plastic wall shadow off its paper backing. Rub it against your hair or a sweater. Press it onto a light-colored wall. The shadows will stay up for days.

Two-Legged Jack-o'-Lantern

microwave-popcorn box ● felt ● two butter boxes ● two large cardboard tubes

1. Cover a microwave-popcorn box with orange felt and decorate it like a jack-o'-lantern. Roll a strip of brown felt to make a stem. Cut green felt leaves. Glue in place.
2. Cover two butter boxes with felt.
3. Trace around a cardboard tube on the butter boxes. Cut out the holes. Using the same tube, trace two circles spaced apart underneath the jack-o'-lantern. Cut out the holes. Place the cardboard tubes in the holes to make legs. Glue in place.
4. Decorate the tubes with felt strips.

Spooky Pin Pal

white felt ● permanent marker ● safety pin

1. Cut two matching ghost shapes from white felt. Glue them together and let them dry.
2. With a permanent marker, draw on the ghost's face and outline the body.
3. Glue a safety pin to the back of the ghost. Then glue a small strip of felt across the opened pin and let it dry.

Clothespin Kitty

two spring-type clothespins ● craft stick ● chenille stick ● wood circle ● wiggle eyes ● construction paper

1. Clip a spring-type clothespin to one end of a craft stick. Bend a black chenille stick into a jagged tail and tuck it between the craft stick and the clothespin. Glue in place.
2. Leave a short length of stick at the other end and glue on another clothespin.
3. For the head, glue a small wood circle on the front of the cat. Paint the cat black. Let dry.
4. Add wiggle eyes and small construction-paper triangles for ears. Let dry.

Puppy Dog Mask

large paper bag ● construction paper ● yarn

1. Cut off 6 inches from the opening of a large paper bag. Glue construction paper to one large side of the bag.
2. From paper, cut out and glue a head and ears, a nose, a mouth, and two eyes. Add yarn whiskers.
3. Put the bag on your head. Have a friend mark with a crayon where the eyeholes should be. Remove the bag and cut out the eyeholes.

Trick-or-Treat Around the Block

pinking shears ● poster board ● metal fastener
● paper plate ● candy corn

1. Using pinking shears, cut out a circle of poster board that is slightly larger than the underside of a paper plate. Color the edge of the circle with orange marker.
2. Divide the circle into eight even wedges. Draw and color a house in each of the sections as shown. Write directions under each of the houses: *Jackpot! Get 5 candies. Move 3 spaces. / Bag ripped. Lose 2 candies. Move 5 spaces. / Getting late. Jump ahead 2 spaces. Spin again. / Share a candy from the pot with everyone. / Flashlight failed. Go to start. Spin again. / Bellyache. Give everyone 1 piece of your candy. Move 4 spaces. / Get 2 candies. Move 2 spaces. / Get 1 candy. Spin again.*
3. With a metal fastener, attach the circle to the center of an upside-down paper plate.
4. Make sixteen "sidewalk" spaces on the edge of the plate as shown. Draw an arrow in the center of each space, pointing toward the spinner. Label START and FINISH on the plate.
5. Cut out and decorate four small circles of poster board for game markers. To play, place the trick-or-treater markers on the sidewalk at the START. Take turns moving and collecting candy corn according to what you spin.

Autumn Leaves Place Mat

white and black construction paper ● leaves
● clear self-adhesive paper

1. Under a faucet, wet one side of a large sheet of white construction paper.
2. With large brushes, drop yellow, green, and red blobs of paint here and there onto the wet paper.
3. Tilt the paper back and forth, keeping it over the sink or tub, until the colors have run across the paper. Let dry.
4. Draw or trace leaf shapes onto a black sheet of paper the same size as the white paper. Cut out each leaf shape.
5. Glue the black paper over the painted paper to see the autumn leaves. Cover the finished place mat with clear self-adhesive paper.

Ghost-in-the-Cup

white paper ● plastic container with snap-on lid ● construction paper ● small plastic-foam ball ● white fabric ● thread

1. Cut white paper to fit around a plastic container. Color the top one-third yellow and the bottom one-third orange. Cut out candy-corn shapes from paper and color them. Glue them to the paper. Glue the paper around the container.
2. Cover the snap-on lid with yellow construction paper. Add a large candy-corn shape to the top. Decorate as shown.
3. Cut two strips of paper 1 inch wide. Fold the strips over each other, as shown in the diagrams, to form a long spring. The spring, when flattened, should rise to the height of the plastic container. Glue one end of it to the inside bottom of the container.
4. Cover a small plastic-foam ball with white fabric, and secure with thread at the neck. Add eyes and a mouth. Spread out the ghost body and glue the bottom of the ball to the other end of the spring.
5. Push the ghost inside the container and close the lid. Surprise a friend by opening the lid. See the ghost pop up and down.

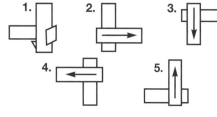

Elephant Mask

four rectangular facial tissue boxes ● masking tape ● plastic gloves ● black and white shoe polish ● cloth ● paper ● paint stirrer

1. Measure 1 inch up from the bottom of three rectangular facial tissue boxes and draw a line. Cut on the line. Discard the tops.
2. Glue two boxes at right angles to one box to form the head. Cut a trunk from the remaining box and glue in place.
3. Cut the side boxes in the shape of ears. Cover the head and the ears with pieces of torn masking tape.
4. Cover your work space and wear plastic gloves. Mix black and white shoe polish together to make a gray color. Wipe the polish on the tape with a cloth.
5. Glue on large paper eyes. Cut out eyeholes. Glue on a paint stirrer.

Gourdy

small gourd ● construction paper ● yarn

1. Wash and dry a small gourd. Cut and glue on pieces of construction paper to create a face on the lower half.
2. Spread a line of glue around the gourd above the face. Cut small pieces of black yarn. Press the yarn into the glue to create hair.
3. Add a loop of yarn for a hanger.

Cat-on-a-Stick

construction paper ● craft stick ● yarn

1. Cut four identical circles from black construction paper. Glue two circles to one side of a craft stick and two to the other side to form the body and head of the cat.
2. Cut ears, eyes, and a mouth from paper and glue them to the head.
3. Glue pieces of black yarn to the face to make whiskers, and add a piece to the back of the cat for a tail.

Jumping Spider

paint stirrer ● poster board ● string ● construction paper ● twist ties

1. Paint a paint stirrer black. Draw and cut out a large circle from black poster board. Cut slits around the outside of the circle.
2. Wrap string around the circle, catching it in the slits, to create a spider web. Tape the ends of the string in place on the back.
3. Tie one end of a length of string to the end of the paint stirrer. Glue this end of the stirrer to the back of the circle, keeping the string loose.
4. To make the spider, draw the head and body shape on brown or black construction paper. Cut this out and use it as a pattern to make a second shape. Lay four twist ties across the body of one spider shape. Tape the centers of these ties to the spider's body. Glue the other spider shape to the first, covering the ties. Bend the ties into legs. Add facial features.
5. Poke a hole in the center of the spider's body. Push the loose string through the hole to the back of the spider. Knot the string and tape it on the back.
6. To play, hold the web by the paint stirrer handle and flip the spider onto the web so that it lands in a standing position.

Bat Mobile

plastic-foam egg carton ● construction paper ● thread ● fallen tree branch ● yarn

1. For each bat, cut two cups from a plastic-foam egg carton and paint them black. Make wings from black construction paper and glue them between the cups.
2. Add pointed ears, hole-punch dot eyes, and a mouth cut from paper.
3. Glue a thread to each bat and tie each one to a fallen tree branch. Tie pieces of yarn to the branch to hang as a mobile.

Cut-Paper Treat Bags

small white paper bags ● construction paper

1. Decorate one side of a small white paper bag with cutout pieces of construction paper. Make goblins, witches, or other creatures. Glue them in place.
2. Place treats inside each bag for your friends.

Witch's Cat

cracker box ● pint-sized milk carton ● felt ● cardboard

1. Cut a cracker box and a pint-sized milk carton down to make square boxes.
2. Cover them with felt, and glue the small box on top of the bigger box.
3. Cut out paws and a tail from cardboard, cover with felt, and glue them in place.
4. Make a black felt cone. Cut a 4½-inch-wide cardboard circle. Cover the circle on both sides with felt. Glue the cone to the circle.
5. Cut out facial features, hat trim, and a bow from felt, and glue them on.

Pocket-Pal Owl

corrugated cardboard ● yarn ● large brown paper bag
● construction paper

1. Cut out a 5-inch-by-8-inch piece of corrugated cardboard. For a hanger, glue yarn to each end of one of the short sides.
2. Cut out a 9-inch-by-5-inch piece from a large brown paper bag. Fold one 9-inch side down an inch and the other 9-inch side up an inch. (See diagram.) Hook one folded edge under the cardboard edge opposite the hanger. Tape the paper in place on the back. Fold the sides of the paper at an angle, as shown in the photo. Tape the sides in place.
3. From construction paper, draw and cut out eyes, a beak, wings, and other features. Glue everything but the wings on the cardboard. Then glue down only the tops of the wings.
4. Hang up the owl near a phone and keep notepaper and pens in the pocket.

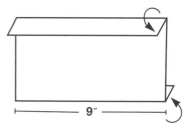

Pumpkin Pin

pumpkin seeds ● fine-point permanent marker
● craft stick ● thin green wire ● toothpick
● hot-glue gun ● safety pin

1. Paint three pumpkin seeds orange. Add gold paint at the point of the seed to make a stem. When dry, add details with a fine-point permanent marker.
2. Ask an adult to help you cut a craft stick to a 2-inch length. Round the ends of the stick and paint it green.
3. Cut a 12-inch length of green wire. Twist the ends together and bend them so that no sharp points are exposed. Twist the wire to make one double-strand length. Wrap the wire around the craft stick as shown. Curl the ends around a toothpick.
4. Glue the seeds to the stick. Let dry.
5. With an adult's help, use a hot-glue gun to fasten a safety pin to the back.

Haunting Puzzle

plastic-foam tray ● paper

1. Cut a large square from the flat part of a plastic-foam tray.
2. Draw a picture on a piece of paper the same size as the plastic square. Glue the picture to the square.
3. When the picture is dry, cut through both the picture and the tray to make the puzzle pieces.

Sponge Jack-o'-Lantern

orange cellulose sponge ● felt ● chenille stick ● flashlight

1. Cut a pumpkin shape from an unused orange cellulose sponge (the kind that has irregular holes).
2. Cut out pieces of felt for the eyes, nose, and mouth, and glue them to the pumpkin.
3. Cut a small piece of chenille stick and loop it to form a stem. Glue it to the top of the pumpkin.
4. Place a flashlight behind the jack-o'-lantern, and watch it glow in the dark.

Three-Headed Monster Mask

four large, heavy paper plates ● yarn ● paper ● poster board ● elastic

1. To make the masks for your hands, cut one large, heavy paper plate in half. Place one of the halves on a whole plate, insides facing each other, and glue together at the rim. This forms a pocket for your hand. Repeat for the second mask. To make the mask for your face, use one plate.
2. Punch holes at the top of each mask, and tie yarn for hair. Add other features with paint, paper, and poster board.
3. To wear the face mask, punch a hole on opposite sides of the plate, and tie a piece of elastic to each hole.

Bat Hat

construction paper

1. Cut a strip of black construction paper long enough to fit around your head. Staple the ends together.
2. Draw and cut out a bat head and bat-wing shapes from black construction paper. Decorate with silver marker.
3. Glue the head shape to the front of the black band. Fold one end of the wings to make little flaps. Glue the flaps to the sides of the band.

White-Rat Screecher Creature

heavy paper ● white film canister ● cotton string ● clear tape

1. Cut out a 3-inch circle of heavy paper. Cut it in half and roll it into a cone just big enough to cover a white film canister's opening. Glue the ends together. Use markers to draw eyes, a nose, and whiskers on the cone.

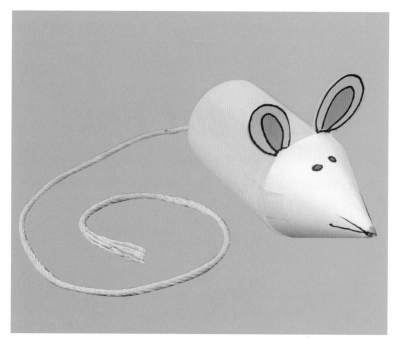

2. Trace and color two ears. Cut them out, leaving a 1/8-inch tab on the bottom of each. Fold the tabs. Add a little glue to each tab and press them on the inside of the cone.
3. Punch a hole in the bottom of the canister. Thread a 12-inch length of cotton string through the hole and make a knot inside the canister.
4. Attach the rat's face to the canister with clear tape.
5. With a little water, wet the string tail thoroughly. Starting near the rat, tightly pinch the string while pulling down on it at the same time to hear it screech.

Witch
Stick Puppet

construction paper ● large craft stick

1. To make the body of the witch, cut pieces of construction paper, and glue them to a large craft stick. Add hands, feet, hair, and facial features cut from paper.
2. Hold the craft stick in your hand and soar your witch through the air.

Friendly
Ghost

paper towels
● cardboard tube
● white paper ● felt

1. Crumple a paper towel into a ball. Stuff it partway into one end of a small cardboard tube so that half is sticking out. This will be the head.
2. Cover the head and tube with a sheet of white paper towel. Use a few dabs of glue to hold the towel to the tube.
3. Cut two hands from white paper. Glue them to the ghost.
4. Cut eyes and a mouth from black felt. Glue them on.

Owl Treat Box

construction paper ● self-adhesive reinforcement rings

1. Draw the owl pattern, as shown, on a square piece of construction paper.
2. Cut out the owl pattern and fold along the dotted lines as shown in the pattern. Tape the sides together to form a box.
3. Add reinforcement rings for eyes. Glue on paper pupils and paper beaks.

Fold on dotted lines.

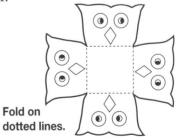

Spider Toss

black film canister ● 1-inch black pompoms ● wiggle eyes ● large box lid ● black yarn

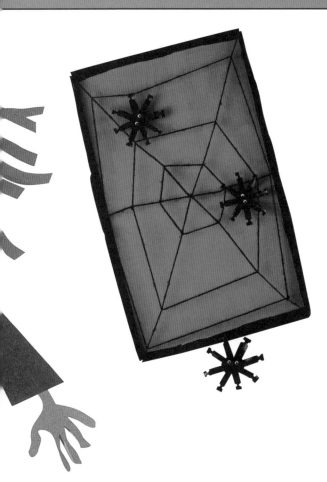

1. To make a spider, warm a black film canister in hot water. This makes the plastic easier to bend. Dry thoroughly. With an adult's help, cut the canister's sides into eight equal sections and bend each backward to look like spider legs. Use a hole punch to make half-circle cuts on each leg.
2. Glue two 1-inch black pompoms to the center of the canister. Glue wiggle eyes to the pompoms. Let dry. Repeat steps 1 and 2 to make more spiders.
3. To make a web, paint a large box lid black and orange. Make six small cuts into the sides of the lid. Wrap black yarn around the box, catching the yarn into the cuts.
4. With another piece of yarn, tie together the yarns that intersect in the center. Tie black yarn to each crosspiece to complete the web. To play Spider Toss, prop the web up against a wall. Gently toss a spider and try to land it on the web.

Hippopotamus Mask

large paper bag ● construction paper

1. Measure down about 6 inches from the opening of a large paper bag, and cut around the entire bag. Set aside the cut section.
2. Using a piece of light-colored construction paper about the same size as one side of the paper bag, draw the opened mouth of a hippopotamus. Color it with crayons and markers.
3. Glue the hippopotamus face to the paper bag. Put the bag on your head. Using a crayon, have a friend carefully mark where the eyeholes should be on the outside of the bag. Remove the bag and cut out the eyeholes.
4. Add cut-paper flowers around the hippopotamus's head. Trim the bag around the bottom of the head and mouth with scissors.

Cat Hang-Up

round cardboard container ● construction paper ● foam paper ● sparkly felt ● sequins ● yarn

1. Cut off the bottom of a round cardboard container. Trim the container to form a cat shape as shown. Paint completely and let dry.
2. Cut features from construction paper, foam paper, and sparkly felt. Glue in place. Add cut sequins for eyes.
3. Punch a hole on opposite sides and in the back of the cat shape, and tie a piece of yarn for a hanger.

Candy-Corn Marker

foam paper ● paint stirrer

1. Cut out an 8-inch-long candy-corn shape from foam paper.
2. Cover the top section with yellow foam paper, the middle section with orange, and the bottom section with white.
3. Glue the candy corn to the paint stirrer and insert it into the ground. Make several to line a walkway.

Ghost Switch Plate

old plastic light-switch plate ● construction paper ● glitter

1. Paint an old plastic light-switch plate black.
2. Draw and cut two ghost shapes from white construction paper. Decorate the ghosts with black glitter and glue.
3. Glue the ghosts to the switch plate. When the glue dries, ask an adult to install the switch plate in your room.

Dancin' Pumpkin

orange and black construction paper ● rubber bands

1. Draw two pumpkins on orange construction paper. Cut them out.
2. Draw four shoes and four mittens on black construction paper. Cut them out.
3. Cut five rubber bands for arms, legs, and a hanger. Tape them to one pumpkin shape. Tape a shoe to each leg and a mitten to each arm. Tape the hanger to the top.
4. Glue the other pumpkin, two shoes, and two mittens over the rubber-band ends on the first set.
5. Use a marker to draw a face.
6. Hold the hanger and make your pumpkin dance, or hang it up and watch it bob and bounce.

Window Buddy

plastic-foam tray ● ribbon ● felt ● crepe paper ● pompoms
● toothpicks ● buttons

1. Cut out a circle from a clean plastic-foam tray. Punch a hole in the edge of the circle and tie ribbon through it for a hanger.
2. Cut out the main parts of your design from felt scraps and crepe paper. Glue them on the circle.
3. Create a face and other details with pompoms, felt, toothpicks, ribbon, and buttons.

Mugsy Mouse

paper ● felt ● needle and thread ● wiggle eyes

1. To create patterns, first draw a mouse body on paper. Make the body taller and wider than your favorite mug. Next draw separate ear, nose, and tail shapes.
2. Use your patterns to cut two of each shape from felt.
3. Glue or sew the body pieces together. Leave the bottom open, and leave a space to add the tail. Glue or sew the tail and the ears to the body. Glue a wiggle eye on each side of the head.
4. For whiskers, glue pieces of thread near the nose.
5. When your mouse is dry, slip it over a mug of cocoa to keep your drink warm.

Web Bracelet

felt ● wide plastic ribbon holder ● yarn ● sequins
● heavy black thread on a spool

1. Glue a piece of white felt around a wide plastic ribbon holder.
2. Cut the body of a spider from felt. Glue on yarn legs. Add sequins for eyes. Glue the spider on the white felt.
3. Tape the end of heavy black thread to the inside of the holder. Holding the spool of thread in your hand, wrap thread around the inside and outside of the holder to look like a spider's web. Cut the thread and tape the end.

Pinecone Owls

fallen tree branch ● plastic food container ● small stones ● clay
● paper ● hemlock pinecones ● plastic food wrap

1. Place a fallen tree branch into a plastic food container filled with small stones and clay. Decorate the outside of the container with paper.
2. To make owls, decorate hemlock pinecones with paper eyes and beaks.
3. Glue the owls to the tree branch. To help hold them in place, wrap a small piece of plastic food wrap around them. Remove the wrap when almost dry.

Meow Mobile

plastic food container ● yarn
● cardboard egg carton ● construction paper

1. For the top section, cut a ring from a plastic food container. Punch four evenly spaced holes near the top of the ring. Insert a piece of yarn through each hole, tying a knot at the end. Gather the four pieces at the top, and tie them together into one knot.
2. Cut out five cardboard egg-carton sections and make them into the shapes of cats' heads as shown. Paint them black. Add whiskers and eyes with paper and glue. Poke a hole in the top of each cat's head.
3. On the bottom of the ring, punch five evenly spaced holes. Thread a piece of yarn through each cat's head and through a hole in the ring. Tie a knot at each end.
4. Glue a piece of black construction paper to cover the back of each head. Add paper ears.

Box-Corner Witch

cereal box ● construction paper

1. Cut a large corner from a cereal box. Cover it with black construction paper.
2. To make the hat brim, cut a circle from black paper. Cut a square hole in the center, and glue it over the point of the box corner.
3. Decorate with facial features, hands, legs, shoes, and a broom made from paper. Glue the legs to the inside edge at the front of the witch.

Happy Jack

poster board ● black construction paper
● thread ● napkin

1. Cut a large ring from poster board and paint it orange.
2. Cut triangles from black construction paper to make the eyes and nose. Tape them to short pieces of thread, and tape the other end of the threads to the back of the ring.
3. Cut a mouth from black paper and glue the bottom to the ring.
4. Glue on a paper stem. Punch a hole to hang the mobile.
5. To make a bow tie, fold a napkin in accordion pleats. Tape it together in the center. Glue it to the pumpkin.

Ghoulish Noisemaker

dried beans ● one-pint milk carton ● construction paper ● yarn ● craft stick

1. Place some dried beans inside a one-pint milk carton, then staple the top closed.
2. Spread glue on the carton, and cover it with construction paper.
3. Make a scary face on one side with cut paper. Staple on yarn at the top for hair.
4. Poke a small hole in the bottom of the carton, and glue a craft stick in the hole for the handle.

Puffy Pumpkin

old tube sock ● cotton balls ● chenille stick ● construction paper

1. Cut an old tube sock in half and fill it with cotton balls. Twist a green chenille stick around the top and curl the ends.
2. Paint the sock orange and the top of the sock green for the stem. Let dry completely.
3. Cut out facial features from construction paper and glue onto the pumpkin. Let dry.

Black-Cat Barrette

barrette ● felt ● embroidery floss ● wiggle eyes

1. Select a barrette that is flat on top.
2. From felt, cut a simple cat that covers the barrette.
3. For the whiskers, tie a few strands of embroidery floss in a knot at the middle. Snip the ends and unravel. For ears, cut two small orange felt triangles. Cut eyes from white felt or use wiggle eyes.
4. Glue everything to the cat. Glue the cat to the barrette. Let dry.
5. Cut out a small square of felt and glue it over the inside of the barrette to secure.

Owl Decoration

construction paper

1. Fold a 3-inch-by-6-inch piece of construction paper in half lengthwise.
2. Starting on the fold, cut 1-inch slits—about ½ inch apart—the entire length of the paper. Open and glue the ends together to form the body.
3. Cut eyes, ears, and a beak from paper. Glue them in place.
4. Cut a strip of paper for a handle, and glue the ends to opposite sides of the owl body. Hang the owl on a doorknob or use it to decorate a table.

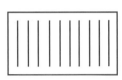

Clown Mask

large paper bag ● construction paper
● large plastic bottle top ● heavy paper plate

1. Cut off 6 inches from the opening of a large paper bag. Set aside the cut section.
2. Put the bag on your head. Using a crayon, have a friend carefully mark where the eyeholes should be on the outside of the bag. Remove the bag. Cut and glue pieces of construction paper to make eyebrows, large eyes with glasses, a nose, a mouth, ears, and a beard. Cut out the eyeholes.
3. Glue a large plastic bottle top to a painted heavy paper plate. Glue on top of the clown's head.

Jack-o'-Pin

frozen-juice pull-top lid ● felt
● foam paper ● safety pin

1. Place a frozen-juice pull-top lid on a piece of felt, and trace around it with a pencil. Do this again and cut out the two circles.
2. Glue one felt circle to each side of the lid.
3. Cut out a mouth, a nose, eyes, and a stem from foam paper, and glue them in place.
4. On the other side, glue or tape a safety pin.

Lion Mask

large, heavy paper plate ● yarn
● felt

1. To make the face, paint the outside bottom of a large, heavy paper plate. Draw and cut out holes for the eyes and a mouth. Decorate with yarn and a red felt tongue.
2. To make the mane, cut pieces of yarn. With the lion's face down, glue the yarn on the rim of the paper plate.
3. Punch two holes close together on each side of the plate rim. Tie a piece of yarn to each hole to hold the mask in place.

Magic Wand

16-inch wooden dowel ● star stickers ● felt
● cotton balls ● glitter

1. For the handle, paint a wooden dowel and let it dry. Add star stickers to the handle.
2. Cut two large identical stars from felt. Spread glue on the edges of the stars.
3. Place a few cotton balls in the center of one star. Lay one end of the handle on top. Place the second star on top of the handle and the first star. Press the stars together at the edges.
4. Spread a thin layer of glue on one side of the star, and sprinkle with glitter. When dry, do the same to the other side.

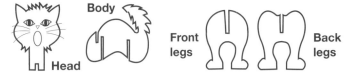

Body   Front legs   Back legs   Head

Cardboard Cat

heavy cardboard

1. From heavy cardboard, cut out the body, front legs, back legs, and head. Make slits in these four parts as shown.
2. Slide the legs and head into the body slits to be sure that the parts fit properly. Take apart.
3. Paint the parts, adding features. Let dry, then put the parts back together.

Cookie Keeper

two heavy paper plates ● cotton balls
● construction paper

1. Paint the outside of one heavy paper plate and let dry.
2. Glue cotton balls on top to make ghosts. Add paper eyes.
3. Cut pieces of construction paper to make a house and pumpkins with cutout faces.
4. Place cookies or other treats on the undecorated paper plate. Use the decorated plate to cover the treats.

Ghostly Treat Box

large cardboard oatmeal container ● construction paper
● white paper ● wooden spool ● cotton ball ● tissue ● thread

1. Cover a large cardboard oatmeal container with black construction paper.
2. From orange paper, cut out four windows and a door. Don't glue them on the container yet.
3. Make tattered shutters from brown paper. Glue them on the windows.
4. Cut out five ghosts from white paper. Add faces to the ghosts, and decorate the door with a marker. Glue the ghosts on the windows and door.
5. Now glue the windows and door onto the container.
6. From orange paper, cut out a circle to fit the lid. Glue it on. For a chimney, cover a wooden spool with black paper. Glue it in place.
7. Place a cotton ball in a tissue, and tie it with thread to make a ghost. Use a marker to add a face. Glue the ghost to the chimney.

Wicked Hat

black poster board

1. Draw a large circle about 14 to 18 inches in diameter on a piece of black poster board. Draw a circle in the center about 5 to 8 inches in diameter. (The size really depends on how large your head is.)
2. Cut out the small center circle. Cut tabs along the inside edge as shown.
3. Draw another circle about 9 to 12 inches in diameter on black poster board. Cut a section from the circle. Roll the section into a cone shape, fitting it over the tabs of the brim.
4. Tape the cone shape together on the inside. Tape the tabs to the inside of the cone.

Cut tabs

Corny Witch

corncob with husk ● dried beans ● poster board
● lightweight cardboard

1. Remove the kernels from a dried corncob and trim the ends. Paint the body black except for the head. Glue on dried beans for eyes, a nose, and a mouth. Trim the cornhusks for the hair.

2. To make the hat, cut two circles from black poster board. Cut the center out of one circle. Cut a slit to the center of the other circle and roll the circle into a cone shape. Glue the cone shape onto the flat circle, covering the hole. Glue the hat to the cornhusk hair.

3. With glue, attach a cardboard base of black feet so that the witch can stand.

Goblin Mask

large paper bag ● rubber band ● yarn
● construction paper

1. Cut through the center of the bottom and along the sides of a large paper bag as shown. Open the flaps. Make fringe with scissors by cutting strips to the folds. Secure the bag below the strips with a rubber band and tie on pieces of black yarn.

2. From construction paper, cut and glue facial features and fringe. With the bag on your head, have a friend carefully mark where the eyeholes should be. Remove the bag and cut out the eyeholes.

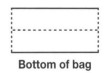

Bottom of bag

Strips of fringe

Rub-On Card

poster board ● colored chalk ● construction paper
● paper towel ● hair spray

1. Draw and cut out a Halloween shape from a piece of poster board. On one side of the shape, rub some colored chalk.
2. Place the shape with the chalk side faceup on the top of a folded sheet of construction paper.
3. With a small piece of paper towel, rub from the center of the chalky shape onto the paper. Lift the shape to see the design on the paper.
4. To keep the picture from smudging, spray it lightly with hair spray. Use the design to decorate a Halloween card.

Leafy Gift Wrap

leaves ● paper

1. Collect some leaves with interesting shapes.
2. Place one leaf upside down on a flat surface. Put a large piece of paper over it. Use a crayon to rub over the leaf to show its veins and edges.
3. Repeat step 2, using different leaves and crayon colors, until the paper is filled with leaves.
4. Color in between the leaf designs.
5. Use the paper to wrap a gift for someone special. Make a card to match.

Craft-Stick Scarecrow

craft sticks ● wood circle ● construction paper
● wiggle eyes ● red permanent marker

1. Overlap two craft sticks lengthwise, one about halfway over the other, and glue in place. Repeat this step with two more craft sticks, and glue the four sticks together side by side. Break one stick in half and glue to the back, about 1 inch from the top, for arms. Glue a wood circle on the front for the head.
2. Paint the body, arms, and legs. Let dry.
3. Cut a hat from brown paper and hair from yellow paper. Glue the hair onto the circle.
4. Glue on the hat and wiggle eyes. Draw a mouth with a red permanent marker. Let dry.

Creepy Spider

chenille sticks ● wooden spool
● beads ● wiggle eyes

1. Cut chenille sticks in half, and stick one end of each half into the center of a wooden spool. Bend the chenille sticks to shape legs.

2. Add two beads to each leg. Paint the spool. Glue on wiggle eyes. Let dry.

Pumpkin-Patch Match

construction paper ● twenty plastic milk-bottle caps
● black permanent marker

1. Cut twenty pumpkin shapes from orange construction paper and glue them onto plastic milk-bottle caps. When dry, draw stems and ridges to each pumpkin. Draw ten pairs of matching shapes on the cap bottoms using a black permanent marker.

2. For the patch, draw four garden rows with pumpkin vines onto a piece of green construction paper.

3. To play, place the pumpkins orange side up in the pumpkin patch. With a friend, take turns turning the pumpkins over two at a time. If the shapes match, keep the pumpkins and take another turn. Otherwise, return them to the patch and let your friend have a turn. The player with the most pumpkins at the end wins.

Nappy Cat

Head

Paws **Tail**

small cardboard tube ● construction paper ● napkin

1. Cut a 1-inch section from a small cardboard tube. Cover it with black construction paper.
2. Draw a head, paws, and tail, as shown, on a piece of black construction paper and cut them out.
3. Decorate the head with features cut from paper. Glue the head, paws, and tail to the tube. Place a rolled napkin through the center.

Wacky Witch

construction paper ● pumpkin ● fabric

1. On construction paper, draw a large circle with a smaller one inside to make the hat brim. Cut out the small circle, cutting tabs along the inside edge of the doughnut shape. To make the hat top, draw a circle on another piece of paper. Cut off about half of the circle and roll it into a cone shape, fitting it over the tabs of the brim and taping in place.
2. Cut strips of paper and tape them inside the hat for hair. Place the hat on top of a pumpkin. Cut out facial features, and attach with rolled pieces of tape.
3. Add a piece of fabric around the witch's neck.

Treat Tote

large cereal box ● half-gallon milk carton
● construction paper ● yarn

1. Cut off the two long top flaps of a large cereal box. Fold back and glue the two small top flaps to each narrow side of the inside of the cereal box. These will be reinforcements for the handle.
2. Cut a half-gallon milk carton in half. Cover the milk carton and the cereal box with glue and black construction paper. Glue them together.
3. Draw and cut out ghost shapes from paper and glue them to the tote box. Add yarn around the top edges.
4. Poke a small hole on each narrow side of the cereal box. Thread the ends of a piece of yarn through the holes from the outside of the box, and tie the yarn into knots on the inside.

"Boo" the Ghost

white plastic-foam tray
● construction paper
● tissue paper

1. Cut a ghost shape and a 3-inch circle from a white plastic-foam tray.
2. Cut the circle in half. Cut two slits in the bottom of the ghost and one on the curved edge of each half circle.
3. Fit the slits in the half circles into the slits in the ghost so it stands up.
4. Decorate the ghost with facial features and a pumpkin made of construction paper. Add a bow tie from tissue paper.

Chain of Pumpkins

construction paper ● permanent marker ● ribbon

1. Stack four or more pieces of orange paper. (The more paper, the more pumpkin shapes and the longer the chain.) Place a pumpkin shape on top of the stack, and cut around it.
2. With a permanent black marker, draw eyes and mouths on the pumpkins. In each pumpkin, cut two vertical slits where the nose should be.
3. Make a pumpkin chain by weaving a long piece of ribbon through the slits in each pumpkin.

Dangling Witch

brown paper bag ● newspaper ● black crepe paper ● yarn ● black poster board

1. Paint a witch's face on the front of a paper bag. Stuff the bag with crumpled newspaper. Fold over the top and glue it shut.
2. For hair, glue strips of black crepe paper on the top of the bag. Attach a long piece of black yarn to the head with staples. Tie a knot in the yarn about 2 inches above the head.
3. Cut a circle of black poster board for the brim of the hat. Make a small hole in the center, and pull the yarn through, letting the brim rest on the knot.
4. To make the top of the hat, roll a piece of black paper into a cone shape. Thread the yarn through the top of the hat and tape the cone shape to the brim.
5. Glue yarn on the hat for a hatband.

Flossie the Ghost

cotton ● facial tissue ● rubber band ● plastic dental floss container ● paper

1. To make the ghost, wrap a small piece of cotton in a facial tissue. Place a small rubber band around the bottom of the tissue ball to form the ghost's neck. Draw a face with a marker.
2. Place the ghost into an empty plastic dental floss container. Tape the back of the ghost's head to the inside lid of the container. Close the lid gently, tucking the head into the box.
3. Decorate the outside of the container with paper to give the ghost a home. Open the lid and the ghost will pop up.

Cat Mask

platter ● poster board ● construction paper ● paint stirrer

1. Cut out a platter shape from a piece of poster board. Cut a slit to the center as shown. Pull one edge of the slit over the top of the other to raise the center slightly. Glue to hold in place.

Cut

2. To make the eyes, cut shapes from construction paper. Glue one on top of the other, and then glue in place on the mask. Cut holes in the center of each paper eye. Add ears, whiskers, and a mouth made from paper. Add a paper bow tie.
3. Glue a paint stirrer to the inside of the mask for a handle.

Light-Bright Jack-o'-Lantern

construction paper ● tissue paper ● string ● paper clip

1. Draw and cut out a pumpkin shape from white construction paper. Cut squares of orange, yellow, and green tissue paper.
2. Place the eraser end of a pencil on the center of a green square of tissue paper. Wrap the ends of the tissue paper up around the pencil and hold them in place. Rub the tissue-paper-covered end of the pencil over a glue stick, then press the pencil onto the pumpkin stem. Remove the pencil so the tissue paper will stick. Continue, using yellow squares to make the facial features and orange for the rest of the pumpkin.
3. Tie the ends of a length of string together to form a loop. Tape the loop to the back of the jack-o'-lantern. Bend a paper clip into a hook and attach the hook to the loop.
4. Hang your jack-'o-lantern on the outside of a lampshade. Switch on the lamp to light up your jack-o'-lantern.

Little Monster

large juice can ● felt ● cardboard

1. Cover the top third of a large juice can with green felt, the middle third a different color, and the bottom third with another color.
2. Cut a circle with two feet from cardboard, cover it with felt, and glue it to the bottom of the can.
3. Add felt arms, facial features, and hair. Add felt details to the body. Roll up two ½-inch strips of gray felt to make bolts and glue them to your monster's neck.

Bread-Dough Necklace

slices of bread ● bowl ● tablespoon ● mixing spoon ● waxed paper ● paper ● table knife ● toothpick ● yarn

1. Remove the crusts from a couple of bread slices. Tear the bread into small pieces and put them in a bowl, add a tablespoon of white glue, and mix together with a spoon. Work the dough into a ball with your hands until it is smooth and elastic.
2. Press the dough out on waxed paper. Draw and cut out a witch or other paper pattern. Place the pattern on the dough and cut around it with a table knife. Make a hole with a toothpick and let the witch dry.
3. Paint details on the witch. When dry, thread a piece of yarn through the hole for a necklace.

Frog Mask

large paper bag ● construction paper

1. Measure about 6 inches from the opening of a large paper bag, and cut around the entire bag. Set aside the cut section.
2. Cover one large side of the paper bag with construction paper, gluing it in place.
3. To make the frog and lily pad, draw and cut pieces from construction paper and glue them in place.
4. Put the bag on your head. Using a crayon, have a friend carefully mark where the eyeholes should be on the outside of the bag. Remove the bag and cut out the eyeholes.

Pumpkin-Patch Toss

five 20-ounce plastic bottles ● tissue paper ● waxed paper ● cardboard ● construction paper ● crepe paper ● eight plastic lids

1. With an adult's help, cut off the bottom section from five 20-ounce plastic bottles.
2. To make the pumpkins, glue pieces of orange tissue paper over the bottle bottoms and brush them with glue for a hard finish. Set them aside to dry on waxed paper.
3. Cut out a large circle from cardboard and cover it with construction paper. Glue the pumpkins, open-side down, to the cardboard base. Leave a space between each pumpkin.
4. Crush five small pieces of green tissue paper into stem shapes. Make vine and leaf shapes from green crepe-paper streamers. Glue them around the pumpkins and base.
5. To make the rings, cut out and discard the center sections of eight plastic lids.
6. To play the game, each player takes a turn throwing all of the rings. Each ring around a pumpkin scores one point. Whoever reaches 20 points first is the winner.

Spooky Brooch

lightweight cardboard ● felt ● small plastic bottle caps ● safety pin

1. Cut a shape from lightweight cardboard. Cover it with glue and a piece of felt. Let dry, and trim around the edge.
2. Glue small plastic bottle caps on top of the felt. Use felt to decorate the bottle caps as holiday characters.
3. Glue or tape a safety pin to the back.

Spooky Scene

construction paper ● tissues ● yarn

1. Fold back the top two corners of a sheet of construction paper to form a crooked-looking roof. Fold the bottom corners under slightly to make crooked walls.
2. Cut the paper to make a doorway and a window with shutters. Fold the door and window open.
3. Cut a crooked chimney and a moon from paper, and glue or tape them in place. Add tissue ghosts in the window and door.
4. Glue on other decorations cut from paper, such as a pumpkin, a tree with folded branches, or a bat.
5. Hang the finished haunted house on your door, using tape or adding a yarn hanger.

Cotton-Top Carl

pumpkin ● cotton balls ● plastic lids ● plastic bottle cap ● teaspoon ● construction paper ● poster board ● chenille sticks ● fabric

1. For hair, brush glue around the top of a pumpkin and press cotton balls into it.
2. On the pumpkin surface, use a pencil to trace around two plastic lids for eyes, a plastic bottle cap for the nose, and a plastic lid for the mouth. Using a teaspoon, dig out shallow holes within the traced circles. Twist the lids and cap into the holes.
3. Cut out pupils from construction paper, and glue them on the eyes. Cut out a mustache shape from poster board, and cover it with cotton. Trim around the edges with scissors if needed. Glue the mustache between the nose and mouth.
4. Twist chenille sticks together to make eyeglasses, and place the earpieces snugly in the hair. Cut two ears from large plastic lids. Have an adult help you cut a slot on each side of the head, and insert the ears. Use a strip of fabric for a bow tie.

Scrappy Witch

cardboard ● felt ● yarn ● buttons ● foam paper

1. From a piece of cardboard, draw and cut out the shape of a witch wearing a hat. Glue on felt for the face, and trim around the edges. To make hair, glue loops of yarn around the witch's face.
2. Glue on black felt for the hat. To make the brim, leave the bottom of the hat unglued and overlapping the hair. Glue on two button eyes and other facial features from foam paper or felt.
3. Decorate the hat with foam or felt cutouts. Glue a loop of yarn to the back of the witch for a hanger.

Scaredy-Cat

black poster board ● metal fasteners
● cardboard egg carton ● foam paper ● stickers

1. Cut a large cat's head, body, and a tail from black poster board.
2. Attach the head and tail to the body with metal fasteners.
3. Cut three cup sections from a cardboard egg carton. Glue two in place for the eyes and one for the nose-mouth area, over the metal fastener. Add a foam-paper nose. Add stickers for eyes.
4. Change the cat's head and tail position anytime you like.

Fabric Ghost

gauze ● old bowl ● spoon ● water ● clear plastic cup ● waxed paper

1. Cut a square of white gauze. Pour some white glue into an old bowl and stir in a little water. Saturate the gauze in the glue-and-water mixture.
2. Set a clear plastic cup upside down on waxed paper. Squeeze out the excess glue from the gauze. Open up the fabric and lay it over the cup to cover. Allow the glue to dry thoroughly.
3. Carefully remove the cup. Use marker to add facial features.

Bat Spinner

chenille stick ● drinking straw ● electrical tape ● construction paper

1. Fold the center of a black chenille stick around a drinking straw, making a loop. Twist the chenille-stick ends together to keep the chenille stick in place. Make sure the loop is loose enough so the chenille stick will slide around the straw.
2. Wrap electrical tape around the straw, above and below the chenille stick loop.
3. Draw and cut a small bat shape from black construction paper. Decorate the bat with silver marker. Tape the bat to the chenille-stick ends.
4. To spin your bat, hold the end of the straw and make a circular movement with your wrist. Your bat will "fly" around the straw.

Haunted Card

construction paper

1. Fold a piece of construction paper in half, then in half again. Draw a house with windows and doors on the front of the card. Cut around three sides of each window and the door so they will open and close.
2. Glue a piece of light-colored paper between the two pages that make up the front of the card. Be careful not to glue the windows and door shut.
3. Open all the windows and the door and write messages behind them or draw scary pictures. Close them up and send your card to a friend.

Finger-Puppet Witch

construction paper ● felt ● yarn ● star stickers

1. Roll and glue together a wide piece of construction paper so your finger will fit inside it. Glue arms to the back.
2. Decorate one side of the paper roll with pieces of felt and yarn to make the face, hat, and hair. Add facial features with a marker.
3. Place star stickers on the witch's dress and hat.

Halloween Sun Catcher

food coloring ● plastic food wrap
● construction paper ● yarn

1. Mix a few drops of food coloring into white glue to make paint. Paint a picture on a piece of plastic food wrap. While it is still wet, cover your painting with another sheet of plastic food wrap. Press the plastic together.
2. Cut strips of construction paper, and glue them around the edges for a frame.
3. Add a loop of yarn to the back for a hanger. Hang the picture in a window where the light will filter through it.

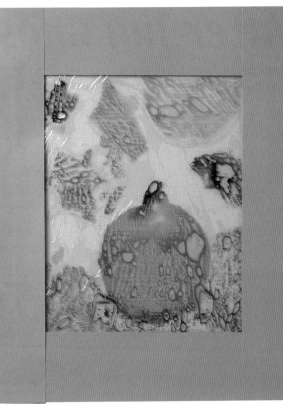

Rabbit Mask

poster board ● headband ● paper clips ● cotton balls
● construction paper ● large paper plate ● yarn ● elastic

1. Fold a piece of white poster board in half. Cut out the ears as shown. Place a headband inside the fold of each ear and glue them together, holding with paper clips until dry. Cover the headband and ears with glue and cotton balls, adding pieces of pink construction paper.

Fold

2. Place a large paper plate in front of your face with the bottom facing out. Using a crayon, have a friend carefully mark on the outside of the plate where the eyeholes should be. Remove the plate and cut out the eyeholes.
3. Draw an outline around the eyes, and draw a nose and a mouth. Cut a tongue from paper and glue in place. Glue on cotton balls, and add yarn whiskers. Staple elastic on opposite sides of the head to hold the mask in place.
4. Cover a round piece of poster board with cotton balls, and tape to the seat of your pants.

Water-Jug Ghost

two one-gallon plastic bottles ● masking tape
● white fabric ● felt

1. With an adult's help, cut the top of a one-gallon plastic bottle so that the second plastic bottle can fit into it when turned upside down.
2. Tape the two bottles together with masking tape.
3. Drape white fabric over the bottles, trim to desired length, and glue it to the jugs in several places.
4. Cut out eyes and a mouth from felt and glue in place.

Triangle Witch

construction paper ● yarn

1. Cut a triangle from black construction paper for the witch's body. Cut a circle from light-colored paper for the head.
2. Use a marker to draw a face. Glue on some yarn hair, and glue the head to the body.
3. Cut a smaller black triangle for the hat and glue it on.
4. Cut a big circle from yellow paper for the moon, and glue it in back of the witch.

Goblin Cup

poster board ● paper ● large craft stick ● plastic-foam cup
● star stickers

1. Cut a goblin head from poster board. Add hair and other features from paper. Glue the head to one end of a large craft stick. Paint the craft stick.
2. Push the other end of the craft stick through the bottom of a plastic-foam cup so the goblin is hiding inside the cup. Add star stickers to the outside of the cup.
3. Hold the stick with one hand and the cup with the other. Make the goblin pop in and out of the cup.

Scarecrow Buddy

three plastic drinking straws
- large craft stick ● felt
- foam paper ● construction paper

1. Cut three plastic drinking straws in half. Glue three pieces to a large craft stick vertically for the body and three horizontally for the arms. Leave space at the top of the craft stick for a head and space at the bottom for feet.
2. Fold a piece of felt in half, and cut out a coat shape. Cut a small slit in the fold for a neck opening, and slip the coat over the body. Glue the coat in place. Add buttons from foam paper.
3. Cut construction paper into thin strips to make straw. Dab with glue, then tuck the strips into the arms, neck, and feet areas.
4. Cut a felt hat and a round piece of felt for the head. Glue in place. Draw on a face with a marker. Add a bird from foam paper.

Tropical-Bird Mask

corrugated cardboard ● paper
- two large craft sticks ● yarn

1. Ask an adult to help you cut out the mask shape and holes for eyes, as shown in the diagram, from corrugated cardboard. Paint one side of the mask, making a beak with a different color.
2. Cut feather-shaped pieces of paper, and glue them around the mask. Roll strips of paper, and glue them around the eyes.
3. Glue two large craft sticks together, overlapping two ends, and let dry. Glue one end to the back of the mask for a handle. Crisscross yarn from one end of the handle to the other and glue in place, leaving the ends hanging down.

Black-and-White Bat

poster board ● string

1. Draw and cut a bat shape from black poster board. Draw and cut half of a bat shape from white poster board. Glue the white half bat to one side of the black bat.
2. Using black marker on the white side and silver marker on the black side, add facial features to your bat.
3. Tie the ends of a length of string together to form a loop. Tape the loop to the back of the bat for a hanger.

Clownin' Around Mask

family-sized cereal boxes ● white paper ● poster board ● pompoms ● yarn

1. Cut off the back and the top sections of a family-sized cereal box. When placed on your head, it should almost touch your shoulders. Cover the box with glue and white paper. Cut out holes for eyes. Cut and glue decorations from poster board. Glue ears to the box sides. Add a pompom nose.
2. Cut and glue loops of yarn to the box top to create hair. Make a hat by cutting out a corner from another box. Decorate it and glue it on top of the hair. Add a pompom on top.
3. Poke a hole in each side of the box behind the ears. Tie a piece of yarn from each hole to hold the mask on.

Ball-o'-Lantern

felt ● basketball ● brown paper bag ● roll of masking tape

1. Draw and cut out a jack-o'-lantern's eyes, nose, and mouth from black felt, and attach them to the basketball with tape.
2. Roll and bend a piece of brown paper bag into a stem. Cut the bottom of the stem into three strips and use strong adhesive tape (not glue) to attach each strip to the top of the basketball to hold the stem in place.
3. Use a roll of masking tape as a stand.

Pumpkin Greeting

heavy paper

1. Cut a sheet of heavy orange paper in half lengthwise. Fold in half. Round off the corners into a pumpkin shape, being careful not to cut off the fold.
2. On the front, cut out the features. Cut a piece of black paper a little smaller than the folded card. Paste it behind the front of the card.
3. Write a message inside. Use the card as an invitation or a greeting card.

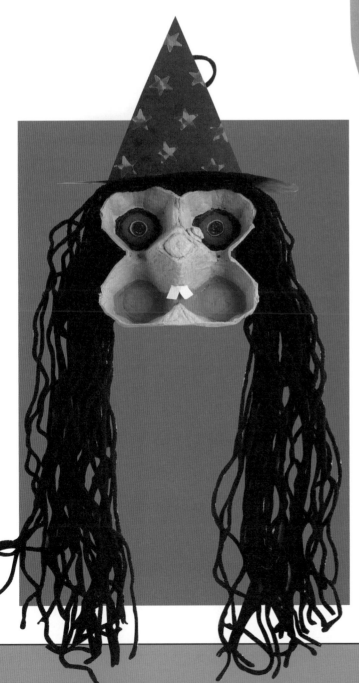

"Egg"-cellent Witch

cardboard egg carton ● construction paper ● yarn ● star stickers

1. For the witch's head, cut four adjoining sections from a cardboard egg carton.
2. Using the inside of the carton as the face, glue on eyes and a mouth from construction paper and a wart from a piece of the egg carton. Glue long pieces of black yarn over the top of the witch's head, letting it hang down around her face.
3. Add a black paper hat to the back of the egg carton. Trim with star stickers.
4. Add a yarn hanger to the back of the witch.

Index